MW01139885

Simple Dessert Trifles

Original recipes by Ethel Richards & Val Walderzak

*I*ntroduction

This recipe book was born out of our passion to make wonderful trifles with great depth of flavor. Trifles are one of the easiest desserts to make, even though they look complicated. With their beautiful layers, trifles make a stunning presentation and are so easy to serve. Simply set this dessert on a table and let guests help themselves!

Whether you're hosting a party or taking a dessert for a pot luck or get-together, these trifles can be made the day ahead. Talk about eliminating last minute preparation and stress!

You'll soon start traditions with special flavors of trifles for holidays, birthdays, showers, picnics and other family and friend gatherings. We hosted a wedding shower for Valerie's daughter whose favorite flavor is banana cream. Hence, Banana Chocolate Trifle was born. We also hosted a baby boy shower for Ethel's daughter-in-law who loves carrot cake. You guessed it! Carrot Cake Trifle was developed.

These recipes are definitely not gender specific. Our husbands have tasted all the recipes, including the flops. They're never too critical because they don't want the trifle test kitchen to stop! They even come up with flavors we should experiment with.

We hope you enjoy these recipes as much as we've enjoyed developing them. One or two ways to garnish each trifle have been shown. These are just examples. Have fun using your own ideas and creativity to garnish these desserts for your special occasions.

Thank you for purchasing our trifle cookbook!

Ethel Richards
Val Walderzak

Contents

1-2	Strategies and Tips
3	Banana Chocolate Trifle
4	Black Forest Trifle
5-6	Blueberry Streusel Trifle
7-8	Caramel Apple Trifle
9-10	Carrot Cake Trifle
11-12	Chocolate Cherry Pistachio Trifle
13	Chocolate Chip Cookie Trifle
14	Dutch Apple Pie Trifle
15	Eggnog Mixed Berry Trifle
16	Individual Strawberry Shortcake Trifles
17	Key Lime Trifle
18	Lemon Gingerbread Trifle
19	Lemon Meringue Pie Trifle
20	Lite Angel Food Berry Trifle
21	Mocha Almond Fudge Trifle
22	Mounds® Bar Trifle
23	Oatmeal Cookie Trifle
24	Oreo® Cookie Trifle
25	Peach Melba Trifle
26	Peanut Butter Cup Trifle
27-28	Pineapple Upside Down Cake Trifle
29-30	Pumpkin Crunch Trifle
31-32	Red Velvet Trifle
33	Rocky Road Trifle
34	S'Mores Trifle
35	Strawberry Cheesecake Trifle
36	Strawberry Creme Trifle
37-39	The Real Stuff (homemade recipes)
40-46	Garnishing Gallery (elaborate decorating ideas)

Strategies and Tips

Trifle Traditions
Consider starting a new tradition for special occasions:
Birthdays
Showers
Holidays
Picnics
Graduations
Weddings
Any family or friend get-together

The ingredients are accessible and the recipes uncomplicated and foolproof. These trifles can be made the day ahead.

Preparing half a recipe makes the perfect amount for a family dinner. Sharing this comfort food with your loved ones could start a new family tradition.

Flavor Strategy
Certain flavors lend themselves to particular holidays, celebrations and seasons:
Great for Spring and Summer - Berry & Lemon Trifles
Think Autumn - Apple, Carrot Cake and Pumpkin Trifles
Perfect for Christmas - Gingerbread, Eggnog, Red Velvet & Strawberry Cheesecake
Valentine's Day - Anything Red
Memorial Day, 4th of July and Labor Day - Blueberry Streusel & Lite Angel Food Berry Trifle (it's red, white & blue)

These are just examples; whatever flavor your family and friends love is perfect any time of the year.

What To Make Trifles In
If you do not wish to make 1 large trifle in a punch bowl or trifle bowl, make individual trifles in the following glassware or clear plastic containers to showcase the layers:
Wine glasses
Cocktail glasses
Champagne flutes
Parfait glasses
Mason jars
Liqueur glasses (shooter size)
Clear plastic glasses

Strategies and Tips

Recipe Flexibility
If you want to lighten or reduce the amount of sugar in any of these recipes, consider using the following:
Sugar free, fat free instant puddings in place of regular puddings
Fat free milk to make the pudding mixture
Fresh fruit instead of canned pie filling
Lite, fat free or sugar free Cool Whip®
Sugar free cake mixes or sugar free cookies

Other Tips
Gluten free cakes and cookies are available and can be used in these recipes.
Use your homemade cake or cookie recipes in place of packaged mixes or purchased items.
Trifles made with brownies, cookies, pound cake, angel food cake, gingerbread or quick bread mixes, make approximately 5 servings less than trifles made with cake mixes.

Garnishing Tips
Consider piping or spooning the top layer of Cool Whip® in a design.
Cool Whip® can be sculpted or feathered with fingers to create an impressive look.
Designs can be drawn on Cool Whip® with fork tines.
When using candles on a trifle (birthday, 4th of July, etc.) it's best to use long candles.
If using sprinkles for garnish, sprinkle at last minute or color will bleed into Cool Whip®.

Lite Angel Food Berry Trifle

Banana Chocolate Trifle
Two Favorite Flavors in One Sensational Creamy Dessert

Ingredients
1   box banana cake mix
1½ cups mini semi-sweet chocolate chips
    (reserve ½ cup for garnish)
1   tablespoon flour
2   3.4 ounce packages banana instant
    pudding
4   cups whole milk
4   bananas sliced into ¼ inch pieces
½   cup orange juice, 7UP® or Sprite®
1   16 ounce container Cool Whip®

Directions
For the cake:
Mix 1 cup chocolate chips with 1 tablespoon flour.
Prepare cake mix according to package directions. At the end of mixing process, add the chocolate chips to the cake batter and continue to mix until incorporated. Bake in any size cake pans you have available according to package directions. Cool and cut into bite size pieces. Save ¼ cup crumbled cake for garnish. This can be done weeks ahead and frozen.

For the pudding:
Prepare the 2 pudding mixes with whole milk, according to package directions.

For the banana slices:
Place banana slices into orange juice, 7UP® or Sprite® for a couple minutes to prevent browning; drain.

In a 25-30 cup glass trifle bowl or punch bowl, layer the ingredients in this order:
½   cake pieces
½   pudding mixture
½   banana slices
½   Cool Whip®
Repeat the process in the same order.

Garnish
Sprinkle most of reserved chocolate chips around edge. Place reserved crumbled cake in center and sprinkle with additional chocolate chips. Refrigerate until ready to serve.

Yield: 15-20 generous 1 cup servings

Black Forest Trifle

This Impressive Dessert Perfectly Pairs Chocolate & Cherries

Ingredients
1   box devil's food cake mix
1½   cups mini semi-sweet chocolate chips (reserve ½ cup for garnish)
1   tablespoon flour
2   21 ounce cans cherry pie filling (reserve ¼ cup for garnish)
2   3.4 ounce packages chocolate instant pudding
4   cups whole milk
1   16 ounce container Cool Whip®

Directions
For the cake:
Mix 1 cup chocolate chips with 1 tablespoon flour. Prepare cake mix according to package directions. At the end of mixing process, add the chocolate chips to the cake batter and continue to mix until incorporated. Bake in any size cake pans you have available according to package directions. Cool and cut into bite size pieces. This can be done weeks ahead and frozen.

For the pudding:
Prepare the 2 pudding mixes with whole milk, according to package directions.

In a 25-30 cup glass trifle bowl or punch bowl, layer the ingredients in this order:
½   cake pieces
1   can pie filling
½   pudding mixture
½   Cool Whip®
Repeat the process in the same order, feathering Cool Whip® with fingers.

Garnish
Sprinkle or grate the reserved chocolate chips on top. Mound the reserved pie filling in the center. Refrigerate until ready to serve.

Yield: 20 generous 1 cup servings

4

Blueberry Streusel Trifle
Grandma's Blueberry Streusel With a Twist

Ingredients

1   16 ounce container Sara Lee® all butter pound cake, or 1 large vanilla pudding cake cut into bite size pieces (the pudding cake will yield more servings)
2   3.4 ounce packages vanilla instant pudding
4   cups whole milk
1½ cups sugar
6   tablespoons cornstarch
¼   teaspoon salt
1⅓ cups water
6½ cups fresh blueberries
    (reserve ½ cup for garnish)
4   tablespoons butter
2   tablespoons fresh lemon juice
1½ cups flour
¼   cup brown sugar
¼   cup granulated sugar
Pinch of salt
1   stick or 8 tablespoons unsalted butter, melted
1   8 ounce container Cool Whip®
1   12 ounce container Cool Whip®

Directions

For the pudding:
Prepare the 2 pudding mixes with whole milk, according to package directions.

For the blueberry pie filling (or use 2 cans blueberry pie filling with 2 cups fresh blueberries):
In large pan, combine 1½ cups sugar, cornstarch and salt. Stir in water and 2 cups blueberries. Cook over medium heat for a couple of minutes until thick. Mix in the butter until melted and remaining blueberries and lemon juice. Cool mixture to room temperature.

For the streusel:
Preheat oven to 400°
Combine 1½ cups flour, ¼ cup brown sugar, ¼ cup granulated sugar and a pinch of salt in a medium bowl; drizzle with the melted butter and toss with a fork until the mixture is evenly moistened and forms pea-sized pieces. Line a rimmed baking sheet with parchment or wax paper. Spread the streusel in an even layer on the paper. Bake the streusel until golden brown, about 5 to 10 minutes. Keep a close watch, streusel will burn easily. Cool.

Blueberry Streusel Trifle

In a 25-30 cup glass trifle bowl or punch bowl, layer the ingredients in this order:

½   cake pieces
½   pudding mixture
½   blueberry pie filling mixture
½   streusel
1   8 ounce container Cool Whip®

Repeat the process in the same order ending with the 12 ounce container Cool Whip®, piped or spread on top.

Garnish
Arrange reserved fresh blueberries on top. Refrigerate until ready to serve.

Yield: 15-20 generous 1 cup servings

Caramel Apple Trifle
An Autumn Taste Sensation Good for Any Season

Ingredients
1   box Duncan Hines® apple caramel cake mix, yellow cake mix or butter recipe cake mix
1   12.25 ounce Smucker's® caramel topping* (reserve 2 tablespoons for garnish)
2   3.4 ounce packages vanilla instant pudding
4   cups whole milk
2   21 ounce cans apple pie filling
1   16 ounce container Cool Whip®

Directions
For the cake:
Prepare and bake cake mix according to package directions. Bake in any size cake pans you have available. Cool and cut or tear into bite size pieces. This can be done weeks ahead and frozen.

For the pudding:
Prepare the 2 pudding mixes with whole milk, according to package directions.

For the pie filling:
Empty apple pie fillings onto a plate and cut apples into bite size pieces.

In a 25-30 cup glass trifle bowl or punch bowl, layer the ingredients in this order:
½ cake pieces
Drizzle ½ caramel topping on cake
½ pudding mixture
½ apple pie filling
½ Cool Whip®
Repeat the process in the same order ending with mounding, piping or spreading Cool Whip® on top. Leave apple filling showing in center, if desired.

Garnish
Drizzle 2 tablespoons reserved caramel topping on top.
Refrigerate until ready to serve.

*Can substitute another brand for Smucker's®

Caramel Apple Trifle

Yield: 20 generous 1 cup servings

A Signature Dessert!

Carrot Cake Trifle

A Favorite Flavor Sure to Please a Crowd

Ingredients
1   carrot cake mix
½   cup chopped pecans
4   ounces cold cream cheese, cubed
2   tablespoons flour
2   3.4 ounce packages
    cheesecake instant pudding
4   cups whole milk
4   tablespoons cornstarch
¾   cup sugar
½   teaspoon salt
2   20 ounce cans crushed pineapple
1   16 ounce container Cool Whip®
1   can sliced pineapple for garnish
Cinnamon for garnish

Yield: 15-20 generous 1 cup servings

Directions

For the cake:
Mix pecans with 1 tablespoon flour. Mix cream cheese with 1 tablespoon flour. Prepare cake mix according to package directions. At the end of the mixing process, add the chopped pecans and cubed cream cheese and continue to mix until incorporated (do not add cubed cream cheese all at once). Bake according to cake mix directions in any size cake pans you have available. Cool and cut or tear into bite size pieces. This can be done weeks ahead and frozen.

For the pudding:
Prepare the 2 pudding mixes with whole milk, according to package directions.

For the pineapple filling:
In heavy saucepan, combine cornstarch, sugar and salt. Add pineapple with juice and mix well. Cook over medium heat until mixture comes to a boil, stirring constantly for about 3 to 5 minutes, or until thickened. Remove from heat and let cool.

In a 25-30 cup glass trifle bowl or punch bowl, layer the ingredients in this order:
½   cake pieces
½   pudding mixture
½   pineapple filling
½   Cool Whip®

9

Carrot Cake Trifle

Repeat the process in the same order ending with mounding, piping or spreading the Cool Whip® on top. Leave pineapple filling showing in center, if desired.

Garnish
Sprinkle cinnamon around the edge of trifle. Cut pineapple slices in fourths and decorate the top. Refrigerate until ready to serve.

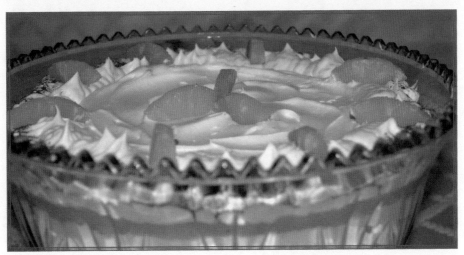

Chocolate Cherry Pistachio Trifle
A Stunning Showpiece!

Ingredients
1   box brownie mix
2   3.4 ounce packages pistachio instant pudding
4   cups whole milk
½   cup chopped pistachios (reserve ¼ cup for garnish)
2   21 ounce cans cherry pie filling
1   16 ounce container Cool Whip®
Chocolate bar for garnish

Directions
For the brownie mix:
Prepare and bake brownie mix in a 9"x 13" pan according to package directions. Cool and cut or tear into bite size pieces. This can be done weeks ahead and frozen.

For the pudding:
Prepare the 2 pudding mixes with whole milk, according to package directions. Mix ¼ cup chopped pistachios into pudding.

In a 25-30 cup glass trifle bowl or punch bowl, layer the ingredients in this order:
½   brownie pieces
½   pudding mixture
1   can cherry pie filling
½   Cool Whip®
Repeat the process in the same order ending with mounding, piping, spreading or sculpting the Cool Whip® with fingers in a design on top.

11

Chocolate Cherry Pistachio Trifle

Garnish
Grate chocolate bar on top and sprinkle with ¼ cup reserved chopped pistachios. For a special touch, add candles for a birthday! Refrigerate until ready to serve.

Yield: 15 generous 1 cup servings

Chocolate Chip Cookie Trifle

America's Favorite Cookie Shines in This Yummy Dessert

Ingredients

2   dozen soft chocolate chip cookies; purchased or your favorite homemade (reserve 2 for garnish)

1   11 to 12 ounce package mini semi-sweet chocolate chips (reserve ½ cup for garnish)

2   3.4 ounce packages white chocolate instant pudding

4   cups whole milk

1   16 ounce container Cool Whip®

Directions

For the pudding:

Prepare the 2 pudding mixes with whole milk, according to package directions.

In a 25-30 cup glass trifle bowl or punch bowl, layer the ingredients in this order:

10 cookies broken into bite size pieces

½   mini chocolate chips

½   pudding mixture

½   Cool Whip®

1   dozen cookies broken into bite size pieces

½   mini chocolate chips

½   pudding mixture

½   Cool Whip®

Garnish

Use cookies, mini chocolate chips and Cool Whip® as desired. Refrigerate until ready to serve.

Yield: 15-20 generous 1 cup servings

Dutch Apple Pie Trifle

A Great Dessert for an Autumn Get-Together

Ingredients
1   box spice cake mix
2   3.4 ounce packages vanilla instant pudding
4   cups whole milk
2   21 ounce cans apple pie filling
1   Dutch apple pie (purchase prepared)
1   8 ounce container Cool Whip®
1   12 ounce container Cool Whip®

Directions
For the cake:
Prepare and bake cake mix according to package
directions. Bake in any size cake pans you have available. Cool and cut or tear into bite size
pieces. Save ½ cup crumbled cake for garnish. This can be done weeks ahead and frozen.

For the pudding:
Prepare the 2 pudding mixes with whole milk, according to package directions.

For the pie filling:
Empty apple pie fillings onto a plate and cut apples into bite size pieces.

For the Dutch apple pie:
Cut Dutch apple pie into bite size pieces.

In a 25-30 cup glass trifle bowl or punch bowl, layer the ingredients in this order:
½   cake pieces
½   pudding mixture
½   apple pie filling
½   Dutch apple pie
8   ounce container Cool Whip®
Repeat the process in the same order
ending with the 12 ounce container
Cool Whip® feathered around the
edge of trifle.

Yield: 20 generous 1 cup servings

Garnish
Sprinkle reserved cake crumbs around edge of trifle. Refrigerate until ready to serve.

Eggnog Mixed Berry Trifle

A Holiday Favorite for Family and Friends

Ingredients
1   box white cake mix
1   cup eggnog
8   tablespoons butter (1 stick), melted
3   large eggs
1½ teaspoons pure vanilla extract
2   3.4 ounce packages white chocolate
    instant pudding
4   cups eggnog
2   21 ounce cans strawberry pie filling
2   6 ounce packages fresh raspberries
    (reserve ½ package for garnish)
1   16 ounce container Cool Whip®
Cinnamon for garnish

Yield: 20 generous 1 cup servings

Directions
For the cake:
Place the cake mix, 1 cup eggnog, melted butter, eggs and vanilla in a large mixing bowl.
Blend with an electric mixer on low speed for 1 minute. Stop the machine and scrape down
the sides of the bowl with a rubber spatula. Increase the mixer speed to medium and beat
2 minutes more. Bake according to cake mix directions in any size cake pans you have
available. Cool and cut into bite size pieces. This can be done weeks ahead and frozen.

For the pudding:
Prepare the 2 pudding mixes with 4 cups eggnog, according to package directions.

For the pie filling mixture:
Mix the 2 cans strawberry pie filling with
the fresh raspberries.

**In a 25-30 cup glass trifle bowl or punch
bowl, layer the ingredients in this order:**
½   cake pieces
½   pudding mixture
½   pie filling mixture
½   Cool Whip®
Repeat the process in the same order.

Garnish
Garnish with reserved fresh raspberries and cinnamon. Refrigerate until ready to serve.

Individual Strawberry Shortcake Trifles
An Easy Casual Presentation

Ingredients
1   16.3 ounce package unbaked refrigerator biscuits
1-2 tablespoons butter, melted
2   tablespoons sugar
2   24 ounce containers frozen, sliced strawberries
    with sugar, thawed
3   cups fresh strawberries, sliced (reserve a few for
    garnish)
2   3.4 ounce packages white chocolate instant pudding
4   cups whole milk
1   12 ounce container Cool Whip®
9 ounce clear plastic cups (15-20)

Directions
For the biscuits:
Place biscuits on
baking sheet and
brush with butter.
Sprinkle sugar on
top and bake according
to package directions. Let cool and cut into small cubes.*

Yield: 15-20 servings

For the strawberry filling:
Mix thawed strawberries with fresh sliced strawberries.

For the pudding:
Prepare the 2 pudding mixes with whole milk,
according to package directions.

In 9 ounce clear plastic cups:
Arrange some strawberry filling in the bottom of a plastic cup. Place cubed biscuits over the strawberries and press down. Put more strawberries over the biscuits. Spoon pudding over the strawberries. Spoon Cool Whip® over the pudding. Repeat with biscuits, strawberries, pudding and Cool Whip®. Spoon a small amount of strawberry mixture on top.

Garnish with more Cool Whip® and a sliced strawberry. Refrigerate until ready to serve.

* You will use approximately $\frac{1}{3}$ of a biscuit for each individual trifle.

16

Key Lime Trifle

A Sensational Taste of the Tropics

Ingredients
1   box yellow cake mix
2   14 ounce cans Carnation®
    sweetened condensed milk
1   cup fresh lime juice
1   tablespoon fresh lime zest
4   cups Cool Whip®
2   6 ounce prepared graham cracker
    crusts, broken into pieces
1   16 ounce container Cool Whip®
Extra limes to zest or slice for garnish

Directions
For the cake:
Prepare and bake cake mix according to package directions. Bake in any size cake pans you have available. Cool and cut or tear into bite size pieces. This can be done weeks ahead and frozen.

For the lime mixture:
Mix condensed milk, lime juice and lime zest until combined. Fold in 4 cups Cool Whip®.

In a 25-30 cup glass trifle bowl or punch bowl, layer the ingredients in this order:
½   cake pieces
½   lime mixture
½   graham cracker crust pieces
½   Cool Whip®
Repeat the process in the same order sculpting Cool Whip® around edge.

Garnish
Garnish with lime zest and/or lime slices. Refrigerate until ready to serve.

Yield: 15-20 generous 1 cup servings

Lemon Gingerbread Trifle

Nostalgic Flavors Combined in a New Way

Ingredients
1   14.5 ounce box gingerbread mix
1¼ cups sugar
3   eggs
1   cup fresh lemon juice
Zest of 1 lemon
½   cup unsalted butter
2   3.4 ounce packages vanilla instant pudding
4   cups whole milk
1   16 ounce container Cool Whip®

Directions
For the gingerbread:
Prepare and bake gingerbread mix according
to package directions. Cool and cut or tear into bite size pieces. Reserve ⅓ cup crumbled
gingerbread for garnish. This can be done weeks ahead and frozen.

For the lemon curd:
In a microwave safe bowl, whisk together the sugar and eggs until smooth. Stir in lemon
juice, lemon zest and butter. Cook in the microwave for one minute intervals, stirring after
each minute until the mixture is thick enough to coat the back of metal spoon, approximately
5 to 6 minutes. Remove from the microwave and cool to room temperature. Cover with
plastic wrap and store in refrigerator if not being used immediately.

For the pudding:
Prepare the 2 pudding mixes with whole milk, according to package directions.

In a 25-30 cup glass trifle bowl or punch bowl, layer the ingredients in this order:
½   gingerbread pieces
½   lemon curd
½   pudding mixture
½   Cool Whip®
Repeat the process in the same order
ending with mounding, piping, spreading
or sculpting the Cool Whip® with fingers
in a design on top.

Garnish
Sprinkle reserved gingerbread crumbs on
top and refrigerate until ready to serve.

Yield: 15 generous 1 cup servings

18

Lemon Meringue Pie Trifle

A Burst of Lemon for Easter, Mother's Day, Luncheons and Showers

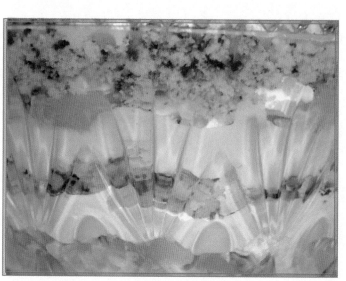

Ingredients
1   16 ounce prepared lemon pound cake or 1 large lemon creme or lemon pudding cake (save 1 cup cake crumbs for garnish)
2   3.4 ounce packages white chocolate instant pudding
4   cups whole milk
1   8 inch prepared lemon meringue pie
1   16 ounce container Cool Whip®

Directions
For the cake:
Cut or tear cake into bite size pieces.

For the pudding:
Prepare the 2 pudding mixes with whole milk, according to package directions.

For the lemon meringue pie:
Cut pie into bite size pieces.

Yield: 15-20 generous 1 cup servings

In a 25-30 cup glass trifle bowl or punch bowl, layer the ingredients in this order:
½   cake pieces
½   pudding mixture
½   lemon meringue pie
½   Cool Whip®
Repeat the process in the same order ending with piping or spooning Cool Whip® around edge to look like meringue.

Garnish
Sprinkle reserved cake crumbs around edge. Refrigerate until ready to serve.

Lite Angel Food Berry Trifle
A Fresh Bright Berry Taste for the Calorie Conscious

Ingredients
1   14 ounce white angel food cake
    (purchase prepared)
1   11.5 ounce jar strawberry Just
    Fruit Spread
1½ tablespoons water
1   3.4 ounce package sugar free,
    fat free white chocolate instant pudding
1   3.4 ounce package sugar free,
    fat free banana cream instant pudding
4   cups fat free milk
6   cups mixed berries (raspberries,
    blueberries and sliced strawberries)
1   16 ounce container lite Cool Whip®
Extra berries for garnish

Yield: 15 generous 1 cup servings

Directions
For the cake:
Cut or tear the angel food cake into bite size pieces.

For the fruit spread:
Mix the fruit spread with water and microwave until loose and syrupy (about 30 seconds).

For the pudding mixture:
Mix together and prepare the 2 pudding mixes with fat free milk, according to package directions.

In a 25-30 cup glass trifle bowl or punch bowl, layer the ingredients in this order:
½   cake pieces
Drizzle with ½ fruit spread
½   pudding mixture
2½ cups berry mixture
½   lite Cool Whip®
½   cake pieces
Drizzle with ½ fruit spread
½   pudding mixture
3½ cups berry mixture
½   lite Cool Whip® mounded or piped
onto berries allowing some berries to show.

Calories per serving: 233

Garnish
Place extra berries on top of Cool Whip® mounds. Refrigerate until ready to serve.

Mocha Almond Fudge Trifle
Mocha Lovers' Delight

Ingredients
1   19.5 ounce box Pillsbury® Mocha
     Fudge Brownie Mix
2   3.4 ounce packages chocolate instant pudding
3 ½ cups whole milk
½   cup very strong cold coffee
1   pound chocolate almond fudge, cut
     into bite size pieces (save half for garnish)*
1   16 ounce container Cool Whip®
Cocoa powder for garnish
Sliced almonds for garnish

Directions
For the brownie mix:
Prepare brownie mix and bake in 9"x13" pan according to package directions. Cool and cut or tear into bite size pieces. This can be done weeks ahead and frozen.

For the pudding mixture:
Prepare the 2 pudding mixes with 3 ½ cups whole milk and ½ cup coffee, according to package directions.

In a 25-30 cup glass trifle bowl or punch bowl, layer the ingredients in this order:
½   brownie pieces
½   pudding mixture
½   fudge pieces
½   Cool Whip®
Repeat the process in the same order ending with mounding, piping or spreading Cool Whip® on top.

Garnish
Dust with cocoa powder. Randomly add cut fudge pieces and sliced almonds. Refrigerate until ready to serve.

*Purchase at local grocery or fudge stores.

Yield: 15 generous 1 cup servings

21

Mounds® Bar Trifle
A Real Chocolate, Coconut Sensation

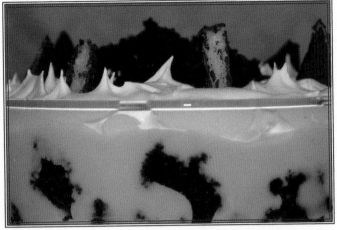

Ingredients
1   box devil's food cake mix
1   cup semi-sweet chocolate chips
1   tablespoon flour
2   3.4 ounce packages white chocolate instant pudding
2   13.5 ounce cans coconut milk
¼   cup whole milk
1   cup sweetened shredded coconut
1   16 ounce container Cool Whip®
Sliced snack size Mounds® bars for garnish

Yield: 15 generous 1 cup servings

Directions
For the cake:

Mix 1 cup chocolate chips with 1 tablespoon flour. Prepare cake mix according to package directions. At the end of the mixing process, add the chocolate chips and continue to mix until incorporated. Bake in any size cake pans you have available according to cake mix directions. Cool and cut or tear into bite size pieces. Crumble enough to make ½ cup and reserve for garnish. This can be done weeks ahead and frozen.

For the pudding mixture:

Prepare the 2 pudding mixes with 2 cans coconut milk and ¼ cup whole milk, according to package directions. Mix sweetened coconut into pudding mixture.

In a 25-30 cup glass trifle bowl or punch bowl, layer the ingredients in this order:
½   cake pieces
½   pudding mixture
½   Cool Whip®
Repeat process in the same order ending with mounding, spreading or sculpting Cool Whip® on top.

Garnish
Place sliced Mounds® bars on top and crumbled cake in center. Refrigerate until ready to serve.

To make Almond Joy® Trifle, follow these same directions adding ½ cup sliced almonds to top.

Oatmeal Cookie Trifle

An Old-Fashioned Cookie Used in a Sophisticated Dessert

Ingredients

2   dozen soft oatmeal cookies with raisins; purchased or your favorite homemade (reserve 2 for garnish)
1   cup white chocolate chips
1   3.4 ounce package white chocolate instant pudding
1   3.4 ounce package butterscotch instant pudding
4   cups whole milk
1   16 ounce container Cool Whip®
Cinnamon for garnish

Directions

For the pudding mixture:
Mix together and prepare the 2 pudding mixes with whole milk, according to package directions.

In a 25-30 cup glass trifle bowl or punch bowl, layer the ingredients in this order:

10   cookies broken into bite size pieces
½   cup white chocolate chips
½   pudding mixture
½   Cool Whip®
1   dozen cookies broken into bite size pieces
½   cup white chocolate chips
½   pudding mixture
½   Cool Whip® mounded around edge and feathered with fingers.

Yield: 15 generous 1 cup servings

Garnish

Cut 2 remaining cookies in quarters. Arrange cookie pieces, points down, on top of Cool Whip®. Sprinkle cinnamon around the edge of trifle. Refrigerate until ready to serve.

Oreo® Cookie Trifle
Cookies and Cream to the Ultimate

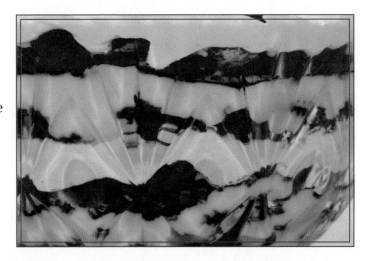

Ingredients
1   box devil's food cake mix
1   cup Hershey's® chocolate flavored syrup
2   3.4 ounce packages white chocolate instant pudding
4   cups whole milk
1   15.5 ounce package original Oreo® Cookies (reserve a few for garnish)
1   16 ounce container Cool Whip®

Directions
For the cake:
Prepare and bake cake mix according to package directions. Bake in any size cake pans you have available. Cool and cut or tear into bite size pieces. This can be done weeks ahead and frozen.

For the pudding:
Prepare the 2 pudding mixes with whole milk, according to package directions.

For the cookies:
Crush cookies into large pieces.

In a 25-30 cup glass trifle bowl or punch bowl, layer the ingredients in this order:
½   cake pieces
Drizzle ½ chocolate flavored syrup on cake
½   pudding mixture
½   crushed cookies
½   Cool Whip®
Repeat the process in the same order and feather Cool Whip® with fingers.

Garnish
Place reserved Oreo® cookies around edge of trifle. Refrigerate until ready to serve.

Yield: 15 to 20 generous 1 cup servings

24

Peach Melba Trifle
An Elegant Dessert for Your Next Garden Party

Ingredients
1   box yellow or butter cake mix
1   10 to 12 ounce jar seedless red raspberry preserves
2   3.4 ounce packages vanilla instant pudding
4   cups whole milk
2   21 ounce cans peach pie filling
2   6 ounce packages fresh raspberries (reserve ½ package for garnish)
1   8 ounce container Cool Whip®
1   12 ounce container Cool Whip®
1   can sliced peaches for garnish

Yield: 20 generous 1 cup servings

Directions
For the cake:
Prepare and bake cake mix according to package directions. Bake in any size cake pans you have available. Cool and cut or tear into bite size pieces. This can be done weeks ahead and frozen.

For the raspberry preserves:
Heat seedless red raspberry preserves in pan or microwave until warm.

For the pudding:
Prepare the 2 pudding mixes with whole milk, according to package directions.

For the peach pie filling:
Empty peach pie fillings onto a plate and cut peaches into bite size pieces.

In a 25-30 cup glass trifle bowl or punch bowl, layer the ingredients in this order:
½   cake pieces
Drizzle ½ warm preserves on cake
½   pudding mixture
½   peach pie filling
½   fresh raspberries
8   ounce container Cool Whip®
Repeat the process in the same order ending with the 12 ounce container Cool Whip®.

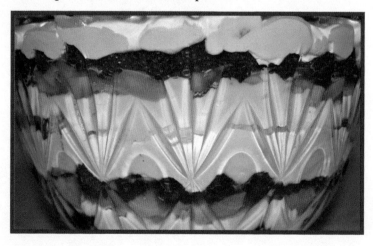

Garnish
Make pinwheel design with peach slices and fresh raspberries. Refrigerate until ready to serve.

Peanut Butter Cup Trifle
Creamy Peanut Butter Enrobed in Chocolate

Ingredients
1   box milk chocolate brownie mix
½   cup creamy peanut butter
2   3.4 ounce packages chocolate
     instant pudding
4   cups whole milk
24 miniature peanut butter cups, chopped
1   16 ounce container Cool Whip®
Additional peanut butter cups for garnish

Directions
For the brownie mix:
Prepare brownie mix according to package directions and pour into a 9x13 pan. Heat peanut butter in microwave for 20 seconds. Drop spoonfuls of peanut butter randomly on brownie batter and swirl with a knife. Bake brownies according to package directions. Cool and cut or tear into bite size pieces. This can be done weeks ahead and frozen.

For the pudding:
Prepare the 2 pudding mixes with whole milk, according to package directions.

In a 25-30 cup glass trifle bowl or punch bowl, layer the ingredients in this order:
½   brownie pieces
½   pudding mixture
½   peanut butter cup pieces
½   Cool Whip®
Repeat the process in the same order ending with piping or mounding the Cool Whip®.

Garnish
Cut additional peanut butter cups in half and randomly place on top. Refrigerate until ready to serve.

Yield: 15 generous 1 cup servings

Pineapple Upside Down Cake Trifle

A Bright New Twist on an Old Fashion Classic

Ingredients

1   box butter cake mix
3   tablespoons cornstarch
¾   cup sugar
½   teaspoon salt
1   20 ounce can crushed pineapple,
      packed in juice
¾   cup chopped maraschino
      cherries
4   tablespoons butter
1   3.4 ounce package vanilla instant
      pudding
1   3.4 ounce package butterscotch
      instant pudding
4   cups whole milk
1   16 ounce container Cool Whip®
Extra maraschino cherries for garnish

Yield: 15-20 generous 1 cup servings

Directions

For the cake:

Prepare and bake the cake mix according to package directions. Bake in any size cake pans you have available. Cool and cut or tear into bite size pieces. This can be done weeks ahead and frozen.

For the pineapple maraschino cherry filling:

In heavy saucepan combine cornstarch, sugar and salt. Add pineapple with juice and mix well. Cook over medium heat until mixture comes to a boil, stirring constantly for about 3 to 5 minutes, or until thickened. Add cherries and stir. Remove from heat and add butter, stirring to melt. Let cool.

For the pudding:

Mix together and prepare the 2 pudding mixes with whole milk, according to package directions.

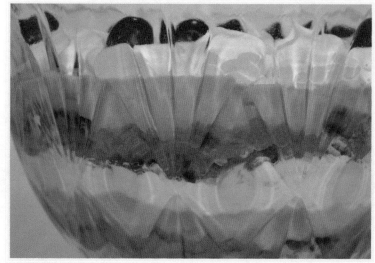

Pineapple Upside Down Cake Trifle

In a 25-30 cup glass trifle bowl or punch bowl, layer the ingredients in this order:

½   cake pieces
½   pineapple maraschino cherry filling
½   pudding mixture
½   Cool Whip®

Repeat the process in the same order ending with mounding or piping the
Cool Whip® on top.

Garnish

Add well drained maraschino cherries on top of the mounded Cool Whip®.
For a birthday, add some candles! Refrigerate until ready to serve.

Pumpkin Crunch Trifle
A Creative Pumpkin Dessert for Your Thanksgiving Crowd

Ingredients
1   box pumpkin bread mix
2   3.4 ounce packages vanilla
    instant pudding
4   cups whole milk
2   8 ounce packages cream cheese,
    room temperature
2   cups powdered sugar
2   cups canned pumpkin
1   teaspoon pumpkin pie spice
28-30 ginger snaps, crushed
1   16 ounce container Cool Whip®
Additional gingersnaps for garnish

Directions
For the pumpkin bread:
Prepare and bake pumpkin bread mix according to package directions. Cool and cut or
tear into bite size pieces. This can be done weeks ahead and frozen.

For the pudding:
Prepare the 2 pudding mixes with whole milk, according to package directions.

For the cream cheese pumpkin mixture:
Beat the cream cheese with mixer until fluffy. Add the powdered sugar, pumpkin and
pumpkin pie spice and continue mixing until combined.

In a 25-30 cup glass trifle bowl or punch bowl, layer the ingredients in this order:
½   pumpkin bread pieces
½   pudding mixture
½   cream cheese pumpkin mixture
½   crushed ginger snaps
½   Cool Whip®
Repeat the process in the same order ending with mounding, piping or spreading the
Cool Whip® on top.

Pumpkin Crunch Trifle

Garnish
Cut and crush additional gingersnaps and garnish as shown in pictures.
Refrigerate until ready to serve.

Yield: 15-20 generous 1 cup servings

Red Velvet Trifle

A Real Showstopper for Christmas, Valentine's Day or 4th of July

Ingredients

1 box white cake mix with pudding
1 cup buttermilk
8 tablespoons butter (1 stick), melted
3 tablespoons unsweetened cocoa powder
3 large eggs
½ teaspoon pure vanilla extract
2 ounces red food coloring
2 3.4 ounce packages white chocolate
  instant pudding
4 cups whole milk
2 21 ounce cans strawberry pie filling
2 6 ounce packages fresh raspberries (reserve
  ½ package for garnish)
1 8 ounce container Cool Whip®
1 12 ounce container Cool Whip®
Cocoa powder for garnish
1 strawberry for garnish, if desired

Yield: 20 generous 1 cup servings

Directions

For the cake:
Place the cake mix, buttermilk, melted butter, 3 tablespoons cocoa powder, eggs, vanilla and red food coloring in a large mixing bowl. Blend with an electric mixer on low speed for 30 seconds. Stop the machine and scrape down the sides of the bowl with a rubber spatula. Increase the mixer speed to medium and beat for 3 minutes. Bake in 9x13 pan for 27 to 29 minutes, until toothpick inserted in center comes out clean. Cool and cut or tear into bite size pieces. This can be done weeks ahead and frozen.

For the pudding:
Prepare the 2 pudding mixes with whole milk, according to package directions.

For the pie filling mixture:
Mix the 2 cans of strawberry pie filling with the fresh raspberries (reserve ½ package for garnish)

In a 25-30 cup glass trifle bowl or punch bowl, layer the ingredients in this order:
½ cake pieces
½ pudding mixture
½ pie filling mixture
1 8 ounce container of Cool Whip®
Repeat the process in the same order ending with mounding, sculpting or spreading the 12 ounce Cool Whip®. Leave strawberry pie filling showing in center, if desired.

Red Velvet Trifle

Garnish

Dust with cocoa powder, if desired, and garnish with reserved berries as shown in pictures. Refrigerate until ready to serve.

Rocky Road Trifle

One of America's Favorite Ice Cream Flavors in a Stunning New Dessert

Ingredients

1   box devil's food cake mix
2   cups milk chocolate chips (reserve 1 cup for garnish)
1   tablespoon flour
2   3.4 ounce packages chocolate instant pudding
4   cups whole milk
¾   cup sliced almonds, chopped
4   cups mini marshmallows (reserve 2 cups for garnish)
1   16 ounce container Cool Whip®
3   tablespoons sliced almonds for garnish

Yield: 15-20 generous 1 cup servings

Directions

For the cake:

Mix 1 cup chocolate chips with 1 tablespoon flour. Prepare cake mix according to package directions. At the end of the mixing process, add the chocolate chips and continue to mix until incorporated. Bake in any size cake pans you have available according to cake mix directions. Cool and cut into bite size pieces. This can be done weeks ahead and frozen.

For the pudding mixture:

Prepare the 2 pudding mixes with whole milk, according to package directions. Mix ¾ cup choppped almonds into pudding.

In a 25-30 cup glass trifle bowl or punch bowl, layer the ingredients in this order:

½   cake pieces
½   pudding mixture
1   cup mini marshmallows
½   Cool Whip®

Repeat the process in the same order.

Garnish

Randomly scatter 2 cups mini marshmallows, 1 cup chocolate chips and 3 tablespoons sliced almonds on top. Refrigerate until ready to serve.

S'Mores Trifle

Not Just for the Campfire Anymore

Ingredients
- 1 box devil's food cake mix
- 1 cup milk chocolate chips
- 1 tablespoon flour
- 3 cups mini marshmallows (reserve 1 cup for garnish)
- 1 12.25 ounce jar marshmallow sundae topping
- 2 3.4 ounce packages white chocolate instant pudding
- 4 cups whole milk
- 14 original flavor graham crackers (reserve 2 for garnish)
- 1 16 ounce container Cool Whip®
- 1 large Hershey's® milk chocolate bar broken into sections for garnish and for grating on top.

Yield: 20 generous 1 cup servings

Directions
For the cake:
Mix chocolate chips with flour. Prepare cake mix according to package directions. At the end of the mixing process, add chocolate chips and continue to mix until incorporated. Bake in any size cake pans you have available according to cake mix directions. Cool and cut into bite size pieces. This can be done weeks ahead and frozen.

For the pudding:
Prepare the 2 pudding mixes with whole milk, according to package directions.

In a 25-30 cup glass trifle bowl or punch bowl, layer the ingredients in this order:
- ½ cake pieces
- 1 cup mini marshmallows

Drizzle ½ jar marshmallow topping
- ½ pudding mixture
- 6 whole graham crackers broken into bite size pieces
- ½ Cool Whip®

Repeat the process in the same order.

Garnish
Randomly place mini marshmallows, chocolate bar sections and graham cracker sections on top. Grate milk chocolate over all garnish ingredients. Refrigerate until ready to serve.

Strawberry Cheesecake Trifle
A Beautiful Layered Dessert

Ingredients
1   box yellow cake mix
1   10 to 12 ounce jar strawberry preserves, warmed (reserve 2 ounces for garnish)
1   prepared Sara Lee® original cheesecake, cut into bite size pieces
2   3.4 ounce packages cheesecake instant pudding
4   cups whole milk
2   21 ounce cans strawberry pie filling
2   cups sliced strawberries
1   8 ounce container Cool Whip®
1   12 ounce container Cool Whip®
3 to 4 sliced strawberries for garnish

Yield: 20 generous 1 cup servings

Directions
For the cake:
Prepare and bake cake mix according to package directions. Bake in any size cake pans you have available. Cool and cut or tear into bite size pieces. This can be done weeks ahead and frozen.

For the pudding:
Prepare the 2 pudding mixes with whole milk, according to package directions.

For the strawberry pie filling mixture:
Mix strawberry pie filling with sliced strawberries.

In a 25-30 cup glass trifle bowl or punch bowl, layer the ingredients in this order:
½   cake pieces
Drizzle ½ warm strawberry preserves
½   cheesecake pieces
½   pudding mixture
½   strawberry pie filling mixture
1   8 ounce container Cool Whip®
Repeat the process in the same order ending with the 12 ounce container Cool Whip®.

Garnish
Drizzle reserved strawberry preserves on top.
Pipe additional Cool Whip® around edge if desired. Add fresh strawberries to center. Refrigerate until ready to serve.

Strawberry Creme Trifle

A Summer Spectacular

Ingredients
1   box white cake mix
Red food coloring
2   3.4 ounce packages white
    chocolate instant pudding
4   cups whole milk
2   large white chocolate bars, grated
2   21 ounce cans strawberry
    pie filling
2   cups sliced strawberries
1   16 ounce container Cool Whip®
3 to 4 sliced strawberries for garnish

Directions

For the cake:
Prepare cake according to package directions and add red food coloring until you reach desired pink color. Bake in any size cake pans you have available according to directions. Cool and cut or tear into bite size pieces. This can be done weeks ahead and frozen.

For the pudding:
Prepare the 2 pudding mixes with whole milk, according to package directions.

For the strawberry pie filling mixture:
Mix the 2 cans of strawberry pie filling with the sliced fresh strawberries.

Yield: **15**-20 generous 1 cup servings

In a 25-30 cup glass trifle bowl or punch bowl, layer the ingredients in this order:
½   cake pieces
½   pudding mixture
½   grated white chocolate
½   strawberry pie filling mixture
½   Cool Whip®
Repeat the process in the same order ending with mounding, piping or sculpting Cool Whip® as shown in picture.

Garnish
Randomly place sliced strawberries on top of Cool Whip®. Refrigerate until ready to serve.

36

The Real Stuff
Homemade Recipes to Use if Desired

Real Whipped Cream (to use in place of Cool Whip®)*
2   cups heavy (whipping) cream, chilled
½   cup powdered sugar
½   teaspoon pure vanilla extract

Place cold heavy cream in a chilled large bowl. Beat with an electric mixer on high speed until thickened, 1 ½ - 2 minutes. Stop the machine and add powdered sugar and vanilla extract. Beat on high speed until stiff peaks form, 1 ½ - 2 minutes.

Make extra if you plan on decorating the top of the trifle with additional whipped cream.

*If using real whipped cream, make the whipped cream and layer the trifle the morning of the party.

Stabilized Whipped Cream (use this recipe if making the trifle a day ahead)
2   tablespoons cold water
1   teaspoon unflavored gelatin
2   cups whipping cream, chilled
½   cup powdered sugar
½   teaspoon pure vanilla extract

In a small bowl, combine water and gelatin. Stir; let stand for 2 minutes. Place the gelatin in the microwave for about 10 to 15 seconds or until dissolved.

Place cold heavy cream in a chilled large bowl. Beat with an electric mixer on high speed gradually adding dissolved gelatin (make sure gelatin is still dissolved when adding). Beat on high speed until thickened, 1 ½ - 2 minutes. Stop the machine and add powdered sugar and vanilla extract. Beat on high speed until stiff peaks form, 1 ½ -2 minutes.

Vanilla Custard (to use in place of vanilla pudding)
1   cup sugar
6   tablespoons cornstarch
½   teaspoon salt
6   egg yolks
4½   cups whole milk
3   tablespoons butter
1   teaspoon vanilla

Bring first 5 ingredients to a boil in a heavy saucepan over medium heat. Whisking constantly, boil approximately 3 to 5 minutes until thickened. Remove from heat and stir in butter and vanilla. Place plastic wrap directly on surface of custard to keep "skin" from forming. Cool and use immediately or refrigerate until ready to use.

The Real Stuff
Homemade Recipes to Use if Desired

Lemon Curd

1¼ cups sugar
3   eggs
1   cup fresh lemon juice
1   lemon, zested
½   cup unsalted butter

In a microwave-safe bowl, whisk together the sugar and eggs until smooth. Stir in lemon juice, lemon zest and butter. Cook in the microwave for one minute intervals, stirring after each minute until the mixture is thick enough to coat the back of metal spoon. Remove from the microwave. Place plastic wrap directly on surface of lemon curd to keep "skin" from forming and cool to room temperature. Store in refrigerator if not being used immediately.

Blueberry Pie Filling

1½ cups sugar
6   tablespoons cornstarch
¼   teaspoon salt
1⅓ cups water
6   heaping cups fresh or frozen blueberries
4   tablespoons butter
2   tablespoons lemon juice

In large pan, combine sugar, cornstarch and salt. Stir in water and 2 cups blueberries. Cook over medium heat for a couple of minutes until thick. Mix in the butter until melted and the remaining blueberries and lemon juice. Cool mixture to room temperature.

Streusel Topping

1½ cups flour
¼   cup brown sugar
¼   cup granulated sugar
Pinch of salt
1   stick or 8 tablespoons unsalted butter, melted

Preheat oven to 400°
Combine the flour, sugars and salt in a medium bowl; drizzle with the melted butter and toss with a fork until the mixture is evenly moistened and forms pea-sized pieces. Line a rimmed baking sheet with parchment or wax paper. Spread the streusel in an even layer on the paper. Bake the streusel until golden brown, about 5 to 10 minutes. Keep a close watch, streusel will burn easily. Cool.

The Real Stuff
Homemade Recipes to Use if Desired

Crushed Pineapple Filling
4   tablespoons cornstarch
¾   cup sugar
½   teaspoon salt
2   20 ounce cans crushed pineapple

In heavy saucepan, combine cornstarch, sugar and salt. Add pineapple with juice and mix well. Cook over medium heat until mixture comes to a boil, stirring constantly for about 3 to 5 minutes, or until thickened. Remove from heat and let cool.

Pineapple Tidbit Filling
2   20 ounce cans pineapple tidbits
¾   cup sugar
½   cup pineapple juice (saved from cans of pineapple tidbits)
4   tablespoons cornstarch

Drain pineapple tidbits and save juice. Cook pineapple tidbits and sugar over low heat until sugar dissolves. Add ½ cup pineapple juice and 4 tablespoons cornstarch; stir and bring to a boil. Remove from heat immediately and cool.

Pineapple Maraschino Cherry Filling
3   tablespoons cornstarch
¾   cup sugar
½   teaspoon salt
1   20 ounce can crushed pineapple, packed in juice
¾   cup chopped maraschino cherries
4   tablespoons butter

In heavy saucepan, combine cornstarch, sugar and salt. Add pineapple with juice and mix well. Cook over medium heat until mixture comes to a boil, stirring constantly for about 3 to 5 minutes, or until thickened. Add cherries and stir. Remove from heat and add butter, stirring to melt. Let cool.

Cream Cheese Pumpkin Filling
2   8 ounce packages cream cheese, softened
2   cups powdered sugar
2   cups canned pumpkin
1   teaspoon pumpkin pie spice

Beat the cream cheese with mixer until fluffy. Add the powdered sugar, pumpkin and pumpkin pie spice and continue mixing until combined.

Garnishing Gallery
For a Big Finish!

FLAGS, FLOWERS & DECORATIONS TO FIT THE OCCASION!

Birthdays

Kids' Birthdays.....Oh What Fun!

Candles, Cakepops, Color

COOKIES, RIBBON... LET YOUR IMAGINATION GO WILD!